PRAISE FOR *Grace Leads, I Follow . . .*

"Lisa Bertsch's meditative, spare language uncovers the vivid,
elemental nature of being human. As she passionately leans
into the inevitable risks of such uncovering, she discovers
that this raw and holy place brings welcome excitement and
more life. Her poems demonstrate that soul, again and then
again, has the power to choose. Bertsch writes in the poem
'Fearless I Stand': 'I beat death back with love.' Such a line
may well serve as nectar in our own journeys!"
—JOHN FOX
AUTHOR OF *Poetic Medicine: The Healing Art of Poem-Making*

"In *Grace Leads, I Follow*, Lisa Bertsch reaches for the divine.
She beseeches, 'Why do you just stand there while my heart
breaks?' and, in the act of making poems, receives prescriptions
to heal 'scarring left by life's lessons.' In reading these gently
insistent missives, the reader shares the journey that has
sustained the writer."

—BARBARA ROCKMAN, AUTHOR OF *Sting and Nest*
WINNER OF THE NEW MEXICO–ARIZONA BOOK AWARD

"Bertsch rings the life bell; talks with wind; prays mountains
and sings the songs of grace and stars. More she brings us along
and in her words we find, 'The warm milk of embodiment /
Our fresh daily gift.' How needed and welcoming her poems are."

—GARY GLAZror
ECT

D0980997

GRACE LEADS, I FOLLOW

GRACE LEADS, I FOLLOW

Poems of Trauma and Transformation

LISA A. BERTSCH

CIELO PUBLISHING

SANTA FE, NEW MEXICO

Published by:

CIELO PUBLISHING
609A Cielo Grande
Santa Fe, NM 87505
www.cielopublishing.com

Editor: Ellen Kleiner

Book design and production: Angela Werneke

Cover art: Angela Werneke, incorporating
"Lotus Flower Floating in Water" © Nataraj, Fotolia

Copyright © 2015 by Lisa A. Bertsch

Printed in the United States of America

PUBLISHER'S CATALOGING-IN-PUBLICATION DATA

Bertsch, Lisa A.

Grace leads, I follow: Poems of trauma and transformation / by Lisa A. Bertsch. -- Santa Fe : Cielo Publishing, [2015]

pages ; cm.

ISBN: 978-0-692-22653-7

Summary: These are poems that arose in response to a traumatic injury and are offered to others facing life-changing events as a source of inspiration and connection.--Publisher.

1. Inspiration--Poetry. 2. Life change events--Poetry.
3. Accidents--Poetry. 4. Chronic pain--Poetry. 5. Traumatic shock--Poetry. 6. Spiritual life--Poetry. 7. American poetry.

PS3602.E76886 S53 2015   2014913225
811/.6--dc23   2014

1 3 5 7 9 10 8 6 4 2

To my family
and all those who help the fallen—
especially those who have touched my life

IN GRATITUDE . . .

My deepest thanks to Dana Moore, my dearest companion; my parents, Mary and Gene Bertsch, who taught me to trust myself; and Ellen Kleiner and Jeanie Williams of Blessingway Authors' Services, as well as Angela Werneke of River Light Media, all of whom got the job done.

*When we walk to the edge of all the light we have
and take a step into the darkness of the unknown,
we must believe that one of two things will happen.
There will be something solid for us to stand on
or we will be taught to fly.*

— Patrick Overton

CONTENTS

INTRODUCTION

POETRY EVOLVED NATURALLY within me in response to a traumatic fall. In the presence of this challenge, both joy and suffering increased in my life in equal proportion. A sense of raw exposure opened my heart as the world around me shifted, becoming more full-bodied and vibrant. A new heart-aching gratitude was implanted within me as I fell in love with life more deeply. Meaning spoke in everything, and all was sacred.

My mind began to weave this meaning into phrases that intrigued me. I wrote them down in a journal, and over time my jumble of jottings became poems. While observing, contemplating, and translating into words the emotions and thoughts from my lightest and darkest times, I refused to lose myself to pain and clung to the vitality of life.

In accepting suffering as well as joy in my daily experience, I have learned to use its rich soil for renewal and growth. As a result, I can now choose again and again to be fully as I am, embracing life in all my human complexity.

Moving in Matter

I am here
Broken or whole—
What does it matter?

In this world
Tossed and turned
One is the other

Equally expanding
Equally confining.

Through action
Thought
Belief
Deed
Choice
Delusion

Reach forth,
Grab something.

Start the beauteous stumbling dance
    of God in flesh—
Moving in matter

Rising
Falling
Breaking
Building
Beginning and ending.

Banished Predictabilities

The leaf fell upward.

Propelled by the wet granite current
It swirled from the deepness of the canyon.

The blackness and its downwardness sent it back up
Unwanted.

Its place is in the heights
The soaring sunlight
The heavens

Despite the predictabilities of gravity and other such things.

In Full Voice Singing

In light eternal I reside.
You cannot take me from this place.
With my feet planted
In full voice singing to God
I cannot hear your calls from the shadows
And fear not your expected advances.

The Cavern of Your Heart

With wringing hands I pace in the cavern of your heart.
Solitary footsteps echo as I call to you,
My voice fracturing and bouncing back
Unfamiliar.

Sickened,
I wonder where you are
And why you do not answer the call of your lost child.

I smile—
Yes, I remember:

You are too close to hear my voice
As you and I have never parted.
My life burns within your boundless walls.
In your heart, I do reside.

Earth of Wonder

Be beauty
Be strength—
In you it is made.

On earth of wonder
Jump up
Bow down
Feel the warm clay.

To turn and pull
Remnants of the past
Formlessly awaiting the new

Be beauty
Be strength—
Glide over brush and bog
On wings of glory
Toward oceans of endless God.

THE CRACK IN REALITY

So sure of what is real—
Blue is blue
And land is firm—

We build walls
With definitions and names
Obscuring the horizon
The fertile beyond
The place of our inception and destiny.

Find the crack in reality
The exception
The definition that defies known laws

Where yellow is blue
And land is light as air.

I Awaken

In the soft breath of morning
Baby blue dreams fade to sunrise,
Sleepy limbs stretch long.

Then to the nest of you I return
Tucking into your downy warmth.

The world seeps in through the
    open window
A wholesome golden tide.
Day begins in a trickle of senses:
I awaken in myself and in you.

Ghosts

All the ghosts you carry,
Those that keep your soul from flight,
Release them from your burdened shoulders

To walk beside you
In lightened load

Where they may speak as wise advisors
Of warnings fair
And aged truths.

Lost Dreams

Lost dreams
Visions
And once-treasured things
Lie rusting in the swamp.

Acres of lowlands
Scattered with desires
Forgotten
Neglected
Abandoned.

Deep scent of decay floats on the lazy breeze.

No life left here—

Only shells and skeletons
Empty
Slithering with snakes.

Thick slime concealing
The lustrous finish of belongings once residing
    in the heart

Now banished in anger
Tossed in with the dented and dinged
Stoves
And old car parts.

A halfhearted drizzle turns to rhythmic sheets
    of rain
Filling the broken porcelain claw-foot tub perched
    on the hilltop
Bathed in a solitary beam of light.

Water washing
Cleansing
The enamel returns,
Polished by remembrances of these once-treasured
    things.

Scavenge and hunt
Dust off your lost dreams.

Allow them to rise
 From the heaps
And reside in the heart yet again.

STILLNESS, STAY

Stillness, stay
I need your comforting depths
To sink into
To be weightlessly suspended
In the sea of your knowing.

Stillness, stay
Your unbiased whisper,
"It will be all right,"
Relaxes the upheaval
In my wounded, wandering
heart.

Stillness, stay
Just a bit longer.
Let me soak,
Infusing my aching humanness
With your reason
Before I go.

Tears at No Pity Café

There is no pity here—
That's why it's safe to cry.

I can have my tears alone
And blot them on my shirt.

With reddened eyes, I order;
The waitress doesn't notice.

The tourists just walk by
Marveling at the menu.

At Dawn

I will rise again at dawn
And lay down past demons and delights
Placing my heart back in the center

As the sun heralds God's reentry
In deep mauve and electric orange
Playing on clouds
Painted on the arched sky.

Before the sun shows her face over the ridge
Speaking in full glory,

I will rise again

And, turning my gaze toward the horizon,
I will step into the day's first light.

CRAVING THE GROUND

Craving the ground
Desiring rest

On fallen knee
I come

And beg your acceptance—

I
Your broken, lost child
Unable to move.

If I Were a Tree

If I were a tree
I'd tell you
You need the earth, just as I do:
The wet sod to root your pale feet
The winds to stir your slumbering soul
The waters in which to immerse and emerge
    a new being
And the fire to warm you in the blackness of
    night.

If I were a tree
I'd beg you to come home:
Mother Earth wails in your absence
Father Sky keeps on searching
Your brothers and sisters,
Earth's other beings,
Miss you in the blessed dance of life.

IN GRACE WE GLIDE

Freed from the pendulum's back and forth
The right and the wrong
Constantly shifting,
A more effortless gait is possible on our walk intertwined.

In grace we glide through the thickness of smoke
Tiptoeing over coals
Without scorching our hearts or tarnishing our souls.

Unscathed
Unbeaten
Stronger
More yielding

We come to a place
Neither above nor below
Just here and then there
As the moments do shift.

Truly tethered to experience
Yet without hands shackled,
Bound by judgment
We reach forth to drink
The warm milk of embodiment,
Our fresh daily gift.

BOULDERS

Boulders rise—
Their soft ruggedness
Guarding me as I walk.

Silent ancestors
Leading the way as landmarks
Offering ancient wisdom.

Earth's first beings—
Grandfather
Grandmother.

I
A descendant of these blessed beings.

I Live on a Mountain Alone

I live on a mountain
Alone.

If I had my way
I would not be here
When you come to visit.

With the birds
I'd be gliding,
Moving on the whim of the wind
Tossed about in her playing.

With the fish
I'd be tumbling,
Hair as seaweed
Slippery body in blue.

With the deer
I'd be running,
Face red with effort
Heart pounding in bouncing laughter.

I live on a mountain
Alone.

If I had my way
I would not be here
When you come to visit.

FROST

Awe-striking luck out of split-second tragedy—
A frost melts to feed the plant it once froze.
I will carry in my bones these aching memories
And I will grow in the new life
The once-frigid water has brought.

CATHEDRAL ARCHES

Cathedral arches
Ceiling of matte lapis lazuli and vibrating golden stars—
Cavernous heights of the mind
Soaring ever heavenward.

Angels fill my head
Dancing and singing
Flitting
Unfurling;
Teeming schools of fish
Slippery
Soaring in God's majestic splendor;

All creation
Circling sound—
Happy holy notes
Light as rain on the gilded breeze.

LIKE LIFE GIVEN BACK

Water permeated my thoughts;
Persistent, it swirled.

My brokenness I bathed in mirages
In veined rivers
Gliding over rocks
Glistening in sunlight

Like life given back.

The desire tasted cool and silky—
Bodies of blue
Depths of green.

My salvation waited in quiet pools
And droplets from the sky.

Empty Love

Perfect
Empty love—
Unasking
Untaking
Given freely with no expiration—
The origin unknowable
Its presence undeniable.

Anywhere but Here

In blackness she rides—
Forest
Glen
Thicket
Anywhere but here.

Steely rhythmed hoofbeats numbing,
Ashen-faced,
Her down-turned heart beats bloody in her gut
Blisters and bruises cascade from her shoulders—
Scarring left by life's lessons.

A maliced party of thieves encircles;
With pounding fists her soul demands.

At her sickening howl, the devils retreat to the
    shadows—
She will not be their meal tonight.

Echoed Alleluias

In worldly daydreams blazing
Broken and bound
We bury our faces in the gravel
At your feet.

In your presence
Hot fleshy waves subside.

In the remaining echoed alleluias
We bathe.
Harsh heartbeat becomes spirit song.

THE ROCKS ON THE SHORE OF THE OCEAN

The rocks on the shore of the ocean . . .

Are they broken souls
Brittle and hardened?
By endless waters pounding
Betrayed and beaten?
In incessant assault
Have they relinquished their power?

Or are they immovable giants of heart
Grateful for the wearing and washing?
Firmly planted,
Sure of their footing?

In rolling foams of blue
Do they yearn to be shaped to perfection?

HEAVEN'S MYSTERY ALOUD

May each being be a song—
The ever-present music of God
Succulent and sweet
Pulsing and pure
A clear bell ringing
Heaven's mystery aloud.

FIELDSTONE

The man who works the soil knows the fieldstone
And with his pained findings builds a sturdy wall.

In his aching back are wisdom and joy
As he knows the spirit's work is his.

The saint and unholy alike
Walk, plant, and weep this way—
Souls entrenched
Hands drenched
In feared compassion rising
For the farmer's hand, although most firm
Requires yet another.

Ascend

Ascend
Ascend—
With all your might
Turn and torque

Shatter the shell
Rise up and out

Reach toward the aboveness that is
    all around.

Sinew and bone
All knowing
A remembering before your time—

Grow large
As you really are,
Filling the periphery
Ribcage expanding
Heart swelling

Your eternal stature bursting within
    your tiny frame.

THE CALLING

The light shines
Hot and mean on my skin.

My eyes dart
Seeking cover—
A comfortable hole
To slink back into

A crevice
To neatly wedge myself within
Where I can become as cool and calcified as
     inert stone.

Finding no refuge
From this grace
This glory
I quake in the beating light

Then
In its permeating presence
I grow still
Allowing the light to flood my being.

NEITHER THIS NOR THAT

Drifting to a doze
All things of matter
Rise and fall

Until they meet
Suspended
In a state of perfection—

The dichotomy merged into sweet unison,

Neither this nor that
Now simply
This and that.

Conversation with the Wind

Saturated air of potentiality
Winding through the canyon
Rises and encircles us
Waking visions that are ours alone,

For each, our wordless conversation with the wind
Knocking us off-balance,
Stimulating momentum to birth new visions.

Go forth
With the wind in your being
Your openness a conduit—
The wind's portal to others.

Languid Blueness

The languid blueness of the predawn sky
Assembles in my bedroom
Calling to court
The magic of a day yet begun,

Filling the air
And my still slumbering soul
With hints and whispers
Of feathered doves
And quivering lilies.

In the haze of morning
Reality rides on divine sorcery
Of which I taste only a drop.

Contented
I yawn
As eternity envelops me—
Creation pulling me into consciousness.

FEARLESS I STAND

Fearless I stand
Dainty wood nymph
Yet mountain soul of a woman.

My tiny feet and slender frame you see
And not the more.
You know nothing of my aged alluvial wisdom—

I beat death back with love.

Fearless I stand
First and evermore God's angel
Christ-light, giggling
Ancient effeminate essence in clay.

WHEN NO WORDS COME

I know
I am struck by a place
A moment
A knowing
When no words come
And no need arises,
When I am spacious like the sea
And nothing else,
When there are no questions,
Only a soft smile in my heart
And ease of breath.

This is when I am most a poet.

Colors Bold

Do not shy from colors bold
Believing in your paleness,
A flower drained in autumn's failing
That never lived in spring.

A soul does speak in palates many
And all things have their place.

These hues brought forth
From gain and wound,
Turn toward them
Every one

And listen with attentive ear,
For each one speaks a truth.

THE SPEED OF LIGHT

Fractured looking-glass
Now a cracked kaleidoscope

Casting broken beams of jeweled light.

Blinding rays crush my eyes
As I try to steady them on my course.

A sea of rainbowed black holes lies before me
Morphing once-identifiable forms.

Motionless
I move at the speed of light
Soaring
Circling
Stalling.

Vast skies slip
Between fast-fumbling fingers.

Mountainous terrain
Quaking under my direct gaze
Crumbles and falls.

In the splintered throbbing light
I attempt to read my surroundings

But blurred unfamiliar landmarks
Provide no direction.

I move forth in faith.

Mountain Prayer

O mountain, what am I to do?
Why do you just stand there while my heart breaks?
Don't you feel the tremors as I do?
Is there no sympathy within you for my human frailty?

In your presence I feel translucent.
I've come to you for solace
But you don't see me here, kneeling in my smallness.

The sunlight washes me away.

WHERE TRUTH IS THE ONLY MATTER

In your loving vastness
I must find my home.

Beyond the earth
Fallacy of firmness

Past notions of career and community
Purpose and pursuit
I go—

Tripping in the blessed mess

Intertwined as vines
Steeped in the story.

Outside the city of man
I arrive
Where the real yet unseen reigns,

Where truth is the only matter.

In My Oatmeal

In my bowl of oatmeal this morning
I found an infinite spiral of spinning stars.

They sang
Smiling in electric blue chaos.

I looked heavenward and knelt.

MURKY WATER

Murky water,
Teach me—
For I must get through before I approach the light
Somersaulting in suspension
Ungrounded yet not rising.

Called back
In a flash from above—
The struggle evaporating

I return to the flow.

Hiding Light

I tell you of the light
Because I've seen it.

It hides like a child
Who hides but is not hidden.

In giddiness
It waits to be discovered.

Coax it from the corner
Back into the center
Where rays can reach
The hidden places—

Light behind the bookcase
Light beneath the rug.

CALDERA

Honey-hued
Baked in sunlight
The soft, feathery grasses sway—

The breeze,
Equal parts September and November,
Warm in sunlight
Cool in the forest.

Glistening frost holding tight in shadows
Regains its dewy nature in the sun's direct gaze.

Grand pines reach into eternity,
A forest so stately it demands adoration.

This place
Complete and whole
Simple and striking.

BLIND RUNNING

Blind running
I dash—
Thorns and twigs scratch and snap.

In the clearing
I collapse,
The harsh rocky earth providing the only comfort I can find.

I lay gasping
With primordial breath
Amongst the prickly pear and scattered crystal,

Sand in my hair
Stuck in the rivulets of tears streaking my face.

Till numbness comes
I cry,
Dispensing every drop of sorrow from my aching bones.

Grace Appears

Where there was only clouded vision
Which grew to timid steps,
Grace appears

Lighting the path upward—
Nudging
Coaxing
Inspiring.

Now dancing the dance
Grace leads,
I follow.

With her hand
I attempt a dance
More splendid
More beautiful
Than I imagined possible
In my mere humanness.

Where I Live

Where I live
Shooting stars race to meet me in the predawn sky
Conflict births miracles
And angel wings carry me godward.

Where do you live?

DEVOTION

Devotion rises
Effortless as ribboned incense

From a soul entirely won
Who has seen all things in her beloved,
Especially her being whole
And truth beyond escape.

Then from a freed and captured heart,
She bows her head
And steps into her fate.

Throwing Sticks

Why do you pace at the shoreline
Throwing sticks into the mud
As the water laps in teasing
At your stubborn toes?

Why do you believe you have no place
When here you are the same as all?

Amidst the reeds and salted wind
Your face reflected liquid blue.

Easter Morning

Early morning—
Crisp
Blunt stillness

Fresh and open
Unformed—
This blessed day begins.

Earthen mystery
Enshrouded in the crystal blueness of the full moon
The scent of frost in shadows lingers
Stars whisper of the beauties of the night past
That they alone have witnessed in their patient vigil.

Playful light skips across the empty pool
From which all wonder and glory arise
Sending ripples to lost souls.

In this timeless moment
Rebirth is inevitable.

Let us each share
In the simple wild audacity of resurrection,
Reclaiming our bodies and spirits
From the frequent deaths we too often allow.

Knit in Infinity

You cannot take my God from me—
Not with your pain
Not with your fear.

We are knit in infinity,
God and I,
In the fragrant mineral earth
In the luminosity of ever-bright stars
In rivulets of tears trembling
In pain's searing freedom
In death and in birth.

As you stand with quaking knees
I root my feet in effervescent love,
Growing fertile
Throbbing in unceasing unity.

ABOUT THE AUTHOR

LISA A. BERTSCH, due in part to her background in visual and performing arts, regards creative expression as a devotional activity. She sings in The Schola Cantorum of Santa Fe, which specializes in sacred a cappella music. She is also a certified yoga teacher with training in adaptive and trauma-sensitive yoga. A native of Pennsylvania, Lisa resides in Santa Fe, New Mexico.